5
american popular piano
TECHNIC

Created by
Dr. Scott McBride Smith

Series Composer
Christopher Norton

Editor
Dr. Scott McBride Smith

Associate Editor
Clarke MacIntosh

Book Design & Engraving
Andrew Jones

Cover Design
Wagner Design

Introduction

Although many books concerned with developing pianistic skills use the word "technique", we prefer to think in terms of "technic". That's because the root word for technic is the ancient Greek tekhnikos – "about art". Think about it. How can you play the piano beautifully without art? And how can you express yourself if you can't control your fingers?

The famous playwright Oscar Wilde said that technic is just another name for personality. He's right. If you don't have a good technic, you will never be able to express your own individuality in your playing. Your ideas may be fresh, your feeling sincere – but if you can't control your fingers, your playing will be lacking.

The theory behind *American Popular Piano Technic* books is simple: provide students with the physical tools for personal expression. Early volumes concentrate primarily on finger technic. But don't forget that you play the piano with your whole body. The fundamentals of good technic are consistent for all levels.

Make sure that:

- ■ your posture is good and that you are sitting correctly.
- ■ your shoulders are down and your arms relaxed.
- ■ your arm is aligned directly behind the note that is playing. Some sideways arm motion will be necessary to achieve this. Many teachers call this "rotation".

- ■ you relax your finger at the bottom of the key. It's not necessary to continue pressing once the note has sounded.
- ■ you repeat each drill many times, listening closely and with concentration. Make sure that it sounds good and feels right.

You may want to proceed through all the exercises in C Major before adding new keys. This is a good idea for some students since the exercises do get a bit harder as they progress. You may want to do each exercise in all keys before moving on. This works too, as long as you don't get bogged down on any one exercise. Which approach works for you? Try both and see.

Does it sound easy? It is – but it takes a lifetime of work to achieve true control and simplicity! Every athlete spends time on drills, exercises and warm-ups outside of the game. Pianists, too, should spend time working on their technic outside of the repertoire pieces. When your piano fundamentals become strong, you will learn more easily and perform more confidently.

Do you want to express yourself in your piano playing? *American Popular Piano Technic* books will help. But they won't work if you don't! Practice carefully and often. Spend time developing your skills – and your skills will help you develop your own personal expression.

Library and Archives Canada Cataloguing in Publication

Smith, Scott McBride

American popular piano [music] : technic / created by Scott McBride Smith ;
series composer, Christopher Norton ;
editor, Scott McBride Smith ; associate editor, Clarke MacIntosh.

To be complete in 11 volumes.
Publisher's nos.: APP T-00 (level P); APP T-01 (level 1); APP T-02 (level 2).
Contents: Preparatory level -- Level 1 -- Level 2.
Miscellaneous information: The series is organized in 11 levels, from preparatory to level 10, each including a repertoire album, an etudes album, a skills book, a "technic" book, and an instrumental backings compact disc.

ISBN 978-1-897379-33-2 (preparatory level).--ISBN 978-1-897379-34-9 (level 1).--ISBN 978-1-897379-35-6 (level 2).--
ISBN 978-1-897379-36-3 (level 3).--ISBN 978-1-897379-37-0 (level 4).--ISBN 978-1-897379-38-7 (level 5)

1. Musical intervals and scales. 2. Piano--Studies and exercises. 3. Musical intervals and scales--Juvenile literature.
4. Piano--Studies and exercises--Juvenile. I. Norton, Christopher, 1953- II. MacIntosh, S. Clarke, 1959- III. Title.

LEVEL 5 TECHNIC
Table of Contents

Introduction ii

Scales & Chords

C Major
Scales 2
Chords 4

G Major
Scales 6
Chords 8

D Major
Scales 10
Chords 12

c harmonic minor
Scales 14
Chords 16

g harmonic minor
Scales 18
Chords 20

A Major
Scales 22
Chords 24

E Major
Scales 26
Chords 28

d harmonic minor
Scales 30
Chords 32

E♭ Major
Scales 34
Chords 36

f harmonic minor
Scales 38
Chords 40

Arpeggios

E♭ Major 42
A♭ Major 43
D♭ Major 44
f♯ minor 45
c♯ minor 46
g♯ minor 47

Mixolydian Modes

C mixolydian mode & licks 48
F mixolydian mode & licks 49
B♭ mixolydian mode & licks 50
G mixolydian mode & licks 51
D mixolydian mode & licks 52
A mixolydian mode & licks 53

Drills

G Major 54
D Major 56
E Major 58
B Major 60
B♭ Major 62
E♭ Major 64
A♭ Major 66
G♭ Major 68

How to Use this Book 70

Technic Tracker .... inside back cover

Scales: C Major

Stop-and-Go Scales

1. Right Hand
   a) What notes does your thumb play? ____ , ____
   b) What note does your 4th finger play? ____

2. Left Hand
   a) What notes does your thumb play? ____ , ____
   b) What note does your 4th finger play? ____

3. Look at Exercise No. 1 below. Fill in the blanks with the correct finger number.

4. Play Exercise No. 1. At each fermata, STOP and say the finger and note name for the next note in the hand that is crossing over or under. For example, in m. 1 pause on beat 2 and say "1 on F", referring to the next note in the RH, then continue to the next fermata (beat 3, m. 1).

Basic Patterns

Play 5x times a day, increasing the speed slightly every day or two, at your teacher's direction.

Complementary Patterns

Play 5x times a day, increasing the speed slightly every day or two, at your teacher's direction.

No. 4   ♩ = 50 - 80

No. 5   ♩ = 50 - 80

No. 6   ♩ = 50 - 80

No. 7   ♩ = 50 - 80

Chords: C Major

Cadences

Chords

Scales: G Major

Stop-and-Go Scales

1. Right Hand

    a) What notes does your thumb play? ____ , ____

    b) What note does your 4th finger play? ____

2. Left Hand

    a) What notes does your thumb play? ____ , ____

    b) What note does your 4th finger play? ____

3. Look at Exercise No. 1 below. Fill in the blanks with the correct finger number.

4. Play Exercise No. 1. At each fermata, STOP and say the finger and note name for the next note in the hand that is crossing over or under. For example, in m. 1 pause on beat 2 and say "1 on C", referring to the next note in the RH, then continue to the next fermata (beat 3, m. 1).

Basic Patterns

Play 5x times a day, increasing the speed slightly every day or two, at your teacher's direction.

Complementary Patterns

Play 5x times a day, increasing the speed slightly every day or two, at your teacher's direction.

No. 4   ♩ = 50 - 80

No. 5   ♩ = 50 - 80

No. 6   ♩ = 50 - 80

No. 7   ♩ = 50 - 80

Chords: G Major

Cadences

Chords

No. 9

No. 10

No. 11

No. 12

No. 13

Scales: D Major

Stop-and-Go Scales

1. Right Hand

  a) What notes does your thumb play? ____ , ____

  b) What note does your 4th finger play? ____

2. Left Hand

  a) What notes does your thumb play? ____ , ____

  b) What note does your 4th finger play? ____

3. Look at Exercise No. 1 below. Fill in the blanks with the correct finger number.

4. Play Exercise No. 1. At each fermata, STOP and say the finger and note name for the next note in the hand that is crossing over or under. For example, in m. 1 pause on beat 2 and say "1 on G", referring to the next note in the RH, then continue to the next fermata (beat 3, m. 1).

Basic Patterns

Play 5x times a day, increasing the speed slightly every day or two, at your teacher's direction.

Complementary Patterns

Play 5x times a day, increasing the speed slightly every day or two, at your teacher's direction.

Chords: D Major

Cadences

Chords

No. 9

No. 10

No. 11

No. 12

No. 13

Scales: c harmonic minor

Stop-and-Go Scales

1. Right Hand
   a) What notes does your thumb play?   ____ , ____
   b) What note does your 4th finger play?   ____

2. Left Hand
   a) What notes does your thumb play?   ____ , ____
   b) What note does your 4th finger play?   ____

3. Look at Exercise No. 1 below. Fill in the blanks with the correct finger number.

4. Play Exercise No. 1. At each fermata, STOP and say the finger and note name for the next note in the hand that is crossing over or under. For example, in m. 1 pause on beat 2 and say "1 on F", referring to the next note in the RH, then continue to the next fermata (beat 3, m. 1).

Basic Patterns

Play 5x times a day, increasing the speed slightly every day or two, at your teacher's direction.

Complementary Patterns

Play 5x times a day, increasing the speed slightly every day or two, at your teacher's direction.

No. 4   ♩ = 50 - 80

No. 5   ♩ = 50 - 80

No. 6   ♩ = 50 - 80

No. 7   ♩ = 50 - 80

Chords: c harmonic minor

Cadences

Chords

No. 9

No. 10

No. 11 (natural minor)

No. 12 (natural minor)

No. 13 (natural minor)

Scales: g harmonic minor

Stop-and-Go Scales

1. Right Hand
   a) What notes does your thumb play?   ____ , ____

   b) What note does your 4th finger play?   ____

2. Left Hand
   a) What notes does your thumb play?   ____ , ____

   b) What note does your 4th finger play?   ____

3. Look at Exercise No. 1 below. Fill in the blanks with the correct finger number.

4. Play Exercise No. 1. At each fermata, STOP and say the finger and note name for the next note in the hand that is crossing over or under. For example, in m. 1 pause on beat 2 and say "1 on C", referring to the next note in the RH, then continue to the next fermata (beat 3, m. 1).

Basic Patterns

Play 5x times a day, increasing the speed slightly every day or two, at your teacher's direction.

Complementary Patterns

Play 5x times a day, increasing the speed slightly every day or two, at your teacher's direction.

Chords: g harmonic minor

Cadences

Chords

No. 9

No. 10

(natural minor)

No. 11

(natural minor)

No. 12

(natural minor)

No. 13

Scales: A Major

Stop-and-Go Scales

1. Right Hand
   a) What notes does your thumb play? ____, ____
   b) What note does your 4th finger play? ____

2. Left Hand
   a) What notes does your thumb play? ____, ____
   b) What note does your 4th finger play? ____

3. Look at Exercise No. 1 below. Fill in the blanks with the correct finger number.

4. Play Exercise No. 1. At each fermata, STOP and say the finger and note name for the next note in the hand that is crossing over or under. For example, in m. 1 pause on beat 2 and say "1 on D", referring to the next note in the RH, then continue to the next fermata (beat 3, m. 1).

Basic Patterns

Play 5x times a day, increasing the speed slightly every day or two, at your teacher's direction.

Complementary Patterns

Play 5x times a day, increasing the speed slightly every day or two, at your teacher's direction.

No. 4 ♩ = 50 - 80

No. 5 ♩ = 50 - 80

No. 6 ♩ = 50 - 80

No. 7 ♩ = 50 - 80

24

Chords: A Major

Cadences

Chords

No. 9

No. 10

No. 11

No. 12

No. 13

Scales: E Major

Stop-and-Go Scales

1. Right Hand
   a) What notes does your thumb play? ____ , ____

   b) What note does your 4th finger play? ____

2. Left Hand
   a) What notes does your thumb play? ____ , ____

   b) What note does your 4th finger play? ____

3. Look at Exercise No. 1 below. Fill in the blanks with the correct finger number.

4. Play Exercise No. 1. At each fermata, STOP and say the finger and note name for the next note in the hand that is crossing over or under. For example, in m. 1 pause on beat 2 and say "1 on A", referring to the next note in the RH, then continue to the next fermata (beat 3, m. 1).

Basic Patterns

Play 5x times a day, increasing the speed slightly every day or two, at your teacher's direction.

Complementary Patterns

Play 5x times a day, increasing the speed slightly every day or two, at your teacher's direction.

No. 4   ♩ = 50 - 80

No. 5   ♩ = 50 - 80

No. 6   ♩ = 50 - 80

No. 7   ♩ = 50 - 80

Chords: E Major

Cadences

Chords

No. 9

No. 10

No. 11

No. 12

No. 13

Scales: d harmonic minor

Stop-and-Go Scales

1. Right Hand
   a) What notes does your thumb play? ____ , ____

   b) What note does your 4th finger play? ____

2. Left Hand
   a) What notes does your thumb play? ____ , ____

   b) What note does your 4th finger play? ____

3. Look at Exercise No. 1 below. Fill in the blanks with the correct finger number.

4. Play Exercise No. 1. At each fermata, STOP and say the finger and note name for the next note in the hand that is crossing over or under. For example, in m. 1 pause on beat 2 and say "1 on G", referring to the next note in the RH, then continue to the next fermata (beat 3, m. 1).

Basic Patterns

Play 5x times a day, increasing the speed slightly every day or two, at your teacher's direction.

Complementary Patterns

Play 5x times a day, increasing the speed slightly every day or two, at your teacher's direction.

No. 4 ♩ = 50 - 80

No. 5 ♩ = 50 - 80

No. 6 ♩ = 50 - 80

No. 7 ♩ = 50 - 80

Chords: d harmonic minor

Cadences

Chords

No. 9

No. 10

No. 11 (natural minor)

No. 12 (natural minor)

(natural minor)

No. 13

Scales: E♭ Major

Stop-and-Go Scales

1. Right Hand

   a) What notes does your thumb play? ____ , ____

   b) What note does your 4th finger play? ____

2. Left Hand

   a) What notes does your thumb play? ____ , ____

   b) What note does your 4th finger play? ____

3. Look at Exercise No. 1 below. Fill in the blanks with the correct finger number.

4. Play Exercise No. 1. At each fermata, STOP and say the finger and note name for the next note in the hand that is crossing over or under. For example, in m. 1 pause on beat 1 and say "1 on F", referring to the next note in the RH, then continue to the next fermata (beat 2, m. 1).

Basic Patterns

Play 5x times a day, increasing the speed slightly every day or two, at your teacher's direction.

Complementary Patterns

Play 5x times a day, increasing the speed slightly every day or two, at your teacher's direction.

No. 4   ♩ = 50 - 80

No. 5   ♩ = 50 - 80

No. 6   ♩ = 50 - 80

No. 7   ♩ = 50 - 80

Chords: E♭ Major

Cadences

Chords

37

No. 9

No. 10

No. 11

No. 12

No. 13

Scales: f harmonic minor

Stop-and-Go Scales

1. Right Hand
   a) What notes does your thumb play? ____ , ____
   b) What note does your 4th finger play? ____

2. Left Hand
   a) What notes does your thumb play? ____ , ____
   b) What note does your 4th finger play? ____

3. Look at Exercise No. 1 below. Fill in the blanks with the correct finger number.

4. Play Exercise No. 1. At each fermata, STOP and say the finger and note name for the next note in the hand that is crossing over or under. For example, in m.1 pause on the "&" of beat 2 and say "1 on F", referring to the next note in the RH, then continue to the next fermata (beat 3, m.1).

Basic Patterns

Play 5x times a day, increasing the speed slightly every day or two, at your teacher's direction.

Complementary Patterns

Play 5x times a day, increasing the speed slightly every day or two, at your teacher's direction.

No. 4 ♩ = 50 - 80

No. 5 ♩ = 50 - 80

No. 6 ♩ = 50 - 80

No. 7 ♩ = 50 - 80

40

Chords: f harmonic minor

Cadences

Chords

No. 9

No. 10

No. 11 (natural minor)

(natural minor)

No. 12

(natural minor)

No. 13

Arpeggios: E♭ Major

No. 1

No. 2

No. 3

Arpeggios: A♭ Major

No. 1

No. 2

No. 3

Arpeggios: D♭ Major

No. 1

No. 2

No. 3

Arpeggios: f♯ minor

No. 1

No. 2

No. 3 (natural minor)

Arpeggios: c♯ minor

No. 1

No. 2

No. 3 (natural minor)

Arpeggios: g♯ minor

No. 1

No. 2

No. 3 (natural minor)

C Mixolydian Mode & Licks

A Mixolydian Mode is a scale that has half steps between scale degrees 3–4 and 6–7. You can think of it as a major scale with a lowered 7th. For example, the "C Mixolydian"

is like a C Major scale, only with a B♭:
1. Start with a major scale;
2. Lower the 7th scale degree a half step.

F Mixolydian Mode & Licks

A Mixolydian Mode is a scale that has half steps between scale degrees 3–4 and 6–7. You can think of it as a major scale with a lowered 7th. For example, the "F Mixolydian" is like an F Major scale, only with an E♭:

1. Start with a major scale;
2. Lower the 7th scale degree a half step.

No. 1

No. 2

No. 3

No. 4

No. 5   No. 6

B♭ Mixolydian Mode & Licks

A Mixolydian Mode is a scale that has half steps between scale degrees 3–4 and 6–7. You can think of it as a major scale with a lowered 7th. For example, the "B♭ Mixolydian" is like a B♭ Major scale, only with an A♭:

1. Start with a major scale;
2. Lower the 7th scale degree a half step.

G Mixolydian Mode & Licks

A Mixolydian Mode is a scale that has half steps between scale degrees 3–4 and 6–7. You can think of it as a major scale with a lowered 7th. For example, the "G Mixolydian" is like a G Major scale, only with an F♮:

1. Start with a major scale;
2. Lower the 7th scale degree a half step.

D Mixolydian Mode & Licks

A Mixolydian Mode is a scale that has half steps between scale degrees 3–4 and 6–7. You can think of it as a major scale with a lowered 7th. For example, the "D Mixolydian" is like a D Major scale, only with a C♮:

1. Start with a major scale;
2. Lower the 7th scale degree a half step.

No. 1

No. 2

No. 3

No. 4

No. 5   No. 6

A Mixolydian Mode & Licks

A Mixolydian Mode is a scale that has half steps between scale degrees 3–4 and 6–7. You can think of it as a major scale with a lowered 7th. For example, the "A Mixolydian" is like an A Major scale, only with a G♮:

1. Start with a major scale;
2. Lower the 7th scale degree a half step.

Drills: G Major

Drawbridge / Rotation Exercises

1. Preparation

Lift your arm about 3 inches above the key without bending at the wrist – as if it were a drawbridge. Flex your starting finger so it feels strong (in m.1, your fifth finger, in m.2 your fourth finger, etc.).

2. Sound Production

a) Play each whole note by dropping into the key, releasing your arm weight with energy. Your wrist should not drop below key level.

b) For each quarter note, without releasing the whole note:
 i.   Rotate toward the finger holding the whole note;
 ii. Rotate back "down" into position, using this motion to create the sound;
 iii. Repeat for each quarter note.

3. Follow Through

Repeat from the beginning on each new whole note.

Upstroke / Inward Rotation Exercises

1. Preparation

Rest your hand on the surface of the keys in good position.

2. Sound Production

a) Play the first note and all the following pickup notes by gently swinging "in" to "stand up" on your thumb. The upward motion creates the sound on the pickup notes.

b) At the same time, rotate your hand towards the thumb to prepare for the accented notes:
 i.   Your thumb position changes from parallel to the key to a comfortably upright position;
 ii. The end of the thumb rotates from the side of the thumb halfway to the tip;
 iii. While the thumb is "standing", the other fingers also lift, opening your hand;
 iv. Relax your hand and arm.

c) "Fall down" to create the sound on the accented notes. You should feel the sensation of falling, dropping, and release.

d) For the accented ♩ notes in mm. 10-11 and 13-14, continue to hold each note as you "stand up" to prepare the next note. Then "fall down" on the next ♩ note to create the sound, as above.

e) Return your hand to level and repeat the process.

No. 4

Upstroke / Outward Rotation Exercises

1. Preparation
Rest your hand on the surface of the keys in good position.

2. Sound Production
a) Play the first note and all the following pickup notes by swinging "in" to "stand up" on your fifth finger. The upward motion creates the sound on the pickup notes.
b) At the same time, rotate your hand towards the fifth finger to prepare for the accented notes:
   i. Your finger position changes from parallel to the key to a comfortably upright position;
   ii. The end of the finger rotates from the pad of the finger almost to the tip;

iii. While the fifth finger is "standing", the other fingers also lift, opening your hand;
iv. Relax your hand and arm.
c) "Fall down" to create the sound on the accented notes. You should feel the sensation of falling, dropping, and release.
d) For the accented ♩ notes in mm. 10-11 and 13-14, continue to hold each note as you "stand up" to prepare the next note. Then "fall down" on the next ♩ note to create the sound, as above.
e) Return your hand to level and repeat the process.

No. 5

No. 6

Drills: D Major

Drawbridge / Rotation Exercises

1. Preparation

Lift your arm about 3 inches above the key without bending at the wrist – as if it were a drawbridge. Flex your starting finger so it feels strong (in m.1, your fifth finger, in m.2 your fourth finger, etc.).

2. Sound Production

a) Play each whole note by dropping into the key, releasing your arm weight with energy. Your wrist should not drop below key level.

b) For each quarter note, without releasing the whole note:
   i. Rotate toward the finger holding the whole note;
   ii. Rotate back "down" into position, using this motion to create the sound;
   iii. Repeat for each quarter note.

3. Follow Through

Repeat from the beginning on each new whole note.

Upstroke / Inward Rotation Exercises

1. Preparation

Rest your hand on the surface of the keys in good position.

2. Sound Production

a) Play the first note and all the following pickup notes by gently swinging "in" to "stand up" on your thumb. The upward motion creates the sound on the pickup notes.

b) At the same time, rotate your hand towards the thumb to prepare for the accented notes:
   i. Your thumb position changes from parallel to the key to a comfortably upright position;
   ii. The end of the thumb rotates from the side of the thumb halfway to the tip;
   iii. While the thumb is "standing", the other fingers also lift, opening your hand;
   iv. Relax your hand and arm.

c) "Fall down" to create the sound on the accented notes. You should feel the sensation of falling, dropping, and release.

d) For the accented ♩ notes in mm. 10-11 and 13-14, continue to hold each note as you "stand up" to prepare the next note. Then "fall down" on the next ♩ note to create the sound, as above.

e) Return your hand to level and repeat the process.

No. 4

Upstroke / Outward Rotation Exercises

1. Preparation
Rest your hand on the surface of the keys in good position.

2. Sound Production

a) Play the first note and all the following pickup notes by swinging "in" to "stand up" on your fifth finger. The upward motion creates the sound on the pickup notes.

b) At the same time, rotate your hand towards the fifth finger to prepare for the accented notes:

  i. Your finger position changes from parallel to the key to a comfortably upright position;

  ii. The end of the finger rotates from the pad of the finger almost to the tip;

  iii. While the fifth finger is "standing", the other fingers also lift, opening your hand;

  iv. Relax your hand and arm.

c) "Fall down" to create the sound on the accented notes. You should feel the sensation of falling, dropping, and release.

d) For the accented ♩ notes in mm. 10-11 and 13-14, continue to hold each note as you "stand up" to prepare the next note. Then "fall down" on the next ♩ note to create the sound, as above.

e) Return your hand to level and repeat the process.

Drills: E Major

Drawbridge / Rotation Exercises

1. Preparation

Lift your arm about 3 inches above the key without bending at the wrist – as if it were a drawbridge. Flex your starting finger so it feels strong (in m.1, your fifth finger, in m.2 your fourth finger, etc.).

2. Sound Production

a) Play each whole note by dropping into the key, releasing your arm weight with energy. Your wrist should not drop below key level.

b) For each quarter note, without releasing the whole note:
   i. Rotate toward the finger holding the whole note;
   ii. Rotate back "down" into position, using this motion to create the sound;
   iii. Repeat for each quarter note.

3. Follow Through

Repeat from the beginning on each new whole note.

Upstroke / Inward Rotation Exercises

1. Preparation

Rest your hand on the surface of the keys in good position.

2. Sound Production

a) Play the first note and all the following pickup notes by gently swinging "in" to "stand up" on your thumb. The upward motion creates the sound on the pickup notes.

b) At the same time, rotate your hand towards the thumb to prepare for the accented notes:
   i. Your thumb position changes from parallel to the key to a comfortably upright position;
   ii. The end of the thumb rotates from the side of the thumb halfway to the tip;

   iii. While the thumb is "standing", the other fingers also lift, opening your hand;
   iv. Relax your hand and arm.

c) "Fall down" to create the sound on the accented notes. You should feel the sensation of falling, dropping, and release.

d) For the accented ♩ notes in mm. 10-11 and 13-14, continue to hold each note as you "stand up" to prepare the next note. Then "fall down" on the next ♩ note to create the sound, as above.

e) Return your hand to level and repeat the process.

No. 4

Upstroke / Outward Rotation Exercises

1. Preparation
Rest your hand on the surface of the keys in good position.

2. Sound Production
a) Play the first note and all the following pickup notes by swinging "in" to "stand up" on your fifth finger. The upward motion creates the sound on the pickup notes.

b) At the same time, rotate your hand towards the fifth finger to prepare for the accented notes:
  i. Your finger position changes from parallel to the key to a comfortably upright position;
  ii. The end of the finger rotates from the pad of the finger almost to the tip;

iii. While the fifth finger is "standing", the other fingers also lift, opening your hand;
iv. Relax your hand and arm.

c) "Fall down" to create the sound on the accented notes. You should feel the sensation of falling, dropping, and release.

d) For the accented ♩ notes in mm. 10-11 and 13-14, continue to hold each note as you "stand up" to prepare the next note. Then "fall down" on the next ♩ note to create the sound, as above.

e) Return your hand to level and repeat the process.

No. 5

No. 6

Drills: B Major

Drawbridge / Rotation Exercises

1. Preparation
Lift your arm about 3 inches above the key without bending at the wrist – as if it were a drawbridge. Flex your starting finger so it feels strong (in m.1, your fifth finger, in m.2 your fourth finger, etc.).

2. Sound Production
a) Play each whole note by dropping into the key, releasing your arm weight with energy. Your wrist should not drop below key level.

b) For each quarter note, without releasing the whole note:
   i. Rotate toward the finger holding the whole note;
   ii. Rotate back "down" into position, using this motion to create the sound;
   iii. Repeat for each quarter note.

3. Follow Through
Repeat from the beginning on each new whole note.

Upstroke / Inward Rotation Exercises

1. Preparation
Rest your hand on the surface of the keys in good position.

2. Sound Production
a) Play the first note and all the following pickup notes by gently swinging "in" to "stand up" on your thumb. The upward motion creates the sound on the pickup notes.
b) At the same time, rotate your hand towards the thumb to prepare for the accented notes:
   i. Your thumb position changes from parallel to the key to a comfortably upright position;
   ii. The end of the thumb rotates from the side of the thumb halfway to the tip;
   iii. While the thumb is "standing", the other fingers also lift, opening your hand;
   iv. Relax your hand and arm.
c) "Fall down" to create the sound on the accented notes. You should feel the sensation of falling, dropping, and release.
d) For the accented ♩ notes in mm. 10-11 and 13-14, continue to hold each note as you "stand up" to prepare the next note. Then "fall down" on the next ♩ note to create the sound, as above.
e) Return your hand to level and repeat the process.

No. 4

Upstroke / Outward Rotation Exercises

1. Preparation
Rest your hand on the surface of the keys in good position.

2. Sound Production

a) Play the first note and all the following pickup notes by swinging "in" to "stand up" on your fifth finger. The upward motion creates the sound on the pickup notes.

b) At the same time, rotate your hand towards the fifth finger to prepare for the accented notes:
   i. Your finger position changes from parallel to the key to a comfortably upright position;
   ii. The end of the finger rotates from the pad of the finger almost to the tip;
   iii. While the fifth finger is "standing", the other fingers also lift, opening your hand;
   iv. Relax your hand and arm.

c) "Fall down" to create the sound on the accented notes. You should feel the sensation of falling, dropping, and release.

d) For the accented ♩ notes in mm. 10-11 and 13-14, continue to hold each note as you "stand up" to prepare the next note. Then "fall down" on the next ♩ note to create the sound, as above.

e) Return your hand to level and repeat the process.

No. 5

No. 6

Drills: B♭ Major

Drawbridge / Rotation Exercises

1. Preparation

Lift your arm about 3 inches above the key without bending at the wrist – as if it were a drawbridge. Flex your starting finger so it feels strong (in m.1, your fifth finger, in m.2 your fourth finger, etc.).

2. Sound Production

a) Play each whole note by dropping into the key, releasing your arm weight with energy. Your wrist should not drop below key level.

b) For each quarter note, without releasing the whole note:
   i. Rotate toward the finger holding the whole note;
   ii. Rotate back "down" into position, using this motion to create the sound;
   iii. Repeat for each quarter note.

3. Follow Through

Repeat from the beginning on each new whole note.

Upstroke / Inward Rotation Exercises

1. Preparation

Rest your hand on the surface of the keys in good position.

2. Sound Production

a) Play the first note and all the following pickup notes by gently swinging "in" to "stand up" on your thumb. The upward motion creates the sound on the pickup notes.

b) At the same time, rotate your hand towards the thumb to prepare for the accented notes:
   i. Your thumb position changes from parallel to the key to a comfortably upright position;
   ii. The end of the thumb rotates from the side of the thumb halfway to the tip;
   iii. While the thumb is "standing", the other fingers also lift, opening your hand;
   iv. Relax your hand and arm.

c) "Fall down" to create the sound on the accented notes. You should feel the sensation of falling, dropping, and release.

d) For the accented ♩ notes in mm. 10-11 and 13-14, continue to hold each note as you "stand up" to prepare the next note. Then "fall down" on the next ♩ note to create the sound, as above.

e) Return your hand to level and repeat the process.

No. 4

Upstroke / Outward Rotation Exercises

1. Preparation

Rest your hand on the surface of the keys in good position.

2. Sound Production

a) Play the first note and all the following pickup notes by swinging "in" to "stand up" on your fifth finger. The upward motion creates the sound on the pickup notes.

b) At the same time, rotate your hand towards the fifth finger to prepare for the accented notes:
   i. Your finger position changes from parallel to the key to a comfortably upright position;
   ii. The end of the finger rotates from the pad of the finger almost to the tip;
   iii. While the fifth finger is "standing", the other fingers also lift, opening your hand;
   iv. Relax your hand and arm.

c) "Fall down" to create the sound on the accented notes. You should feel the sensation of falling, dropping, and release.

d) For the accented ♩ notes in mm. 10-11 and 13-14, continue to hold each note as you "stand up" to prepare the next note. Then "fall down" on the next ♩ note to create the sound, as above.

e) Return your hand to level and repeat the process.

Drills: E♭ Major

Drawbridge / Rotation Exercises

1. Preparation

Lift your arm about 3 inches above the key without bending at the wrist – as if it were a drawbridge. Flex your starting finger so it feels strong (in m.1, your fifth finger, in m.2 your fourth finger, etc.).

2. Sound Production

a) Play each whole note by dropping into the key, releasing your arm weight with energy. Your wrist should not drop below key level.

b) For each quarter note, without releasing the whole note:
   i. Rotate toward the finger holding the whole note;
   ii. Rotate back "down" into position, using this motion to create the sound;
   iii. Repeat for each quarter note.

3. Follow Through

Repeat from the beginning on each new whole note.

Upstroke / Inward Rotation Exercises

1. Preparation

Rest your hand on the surface of the keys in good position.

2. Sound Production

a) Play the first note and all the following pickup notes by gently swinging "in" to "stand up" on your thumb. The upward motion creates the sound on the pickup notes.

b) At the same time, rotate your hand towards the thumb to prepare for the accented notes:
   i. Your thumb position changes from parallel to the key to a comfortably upright position;
   ii. The end of the thumb rotates from the side of the thumb halfway to the tip;
   iii. While the thumb is "standing", the other fingers also lift, opening your hand;
   iv. Relax your hand and arm.

c) "Fall down" to create the sound on the accented notes. You should feel the sensation of falling, dropping, and release.

d) For the accented ♩ notes in mm. 10-11 and 13-14, continue to hold each note as you "stand up" to prepare the next note. Then "fall down" on the next ♩ note to create the sound, as above.

e) Return your hand to level and repeat the process.

No. 4

Upstroke / Outward Rotation Exercises

1. Preparation
Rest your hand on the surface of the keys in good position.

2. Sound Production

a) Play the first note and all the following pickup notes by swinging "in" to "stand up" on your fifth finger. The upward motion creates the sound on the pickup notes.

b) At the same time, rotate your hand towards the fifth finger to prepare for the accented notes:
   i. Your finger position changes from parallel to the key to a comfortably upright position;
   ii. The end of the finger rotates from the pad of the finger almost to the tip;

   iii. While the fifth finger is "standing", the other fingers also lift, opening your hand;
   iv. Relax your hand and arm.

c) "Fall down" to create the sound on the accented notes. You should feel the sensation of falling, dropping, and release.

d) For the accented ♩ notes in mm. 10-11 and 13-14, continue to hold each note as you "stand up" to prepare the next note. Then "fall down" on the next ♩ note to create the sound, as above.

e) Return your hand to level and repeat the process.

No. 5

No. 6

Drills: A♭ Major

Drawbridge / Rotation Exercises

1. Preparation

Lift your arm about 3 inches above the key without bending at the wrist – as if it were a drawbridge. Flex your starting finger so it feels strong (in m.1, your fifth finger, in m.2 your fourth finger, etc.).

2. Sound Production

a) Play each whole note by dropping into the key, releasing your arm weight with energy. Your wrist should not drop below key level.

b) For each quarter note, without releasing the whole note:
   i.   Rotate toward the finger holding the whole note;
   ii. Rotate back "down" into position, using this motion to create the sound;
   iii. Repeat for each quarter note.

3. Follow Through

Repeat from the beginning on each new whole note.

Upstroke / Inward Rotation Exercises

1. Preparation

Rest your hand on the surface of the keys in good position.

2. Sound Production

a) Play the first note and all the following pickup notes by gently swinging "in" to "stand up" on your thumb. The upward motion creates the sound on the pickup notes.

b) At the same time, rotate your hand towards the thumb to prepare for the accented notes:
   i.   Your thumb position changes from parallel to the key to a comfortably upright position;
   ii. The end of the thumb rotates from the side of the thumb halfway to the tip;

   iii. While the thumb is "standing", the other fingers also lift, opening your hand;
   iv. Relax your hand and arm.

c) "Fall down" to create the sound on the accented notes. You should feel the sensation of falling, dropping, and release.

d) For the accented ♩ notes in mm. 10-11 and 13-14, continue to hold each note as you "stand up" to prepare the next note. Then "fall down" on the next ♩ note to create the sound, as above.

e) Return your hand to level and repeat the process.

No. 4

Upstroke / Outward Rotation Exercises

1. Preparation
Rest your hand on the surface of the keys in good position.

2. Sound Production
a) Play the first note and all the following pickup notes by swinging "in" to "stand up" on your fifth finger. The upward motion creates the sound on the pickup notes.

b) At the same time, rotate your hand towards the fifth finger to prepare for the accented notes:
   i. Your finger position changes from parallel to the key to a comfortably upright position;
   ii. The end of the finger rotates from the pad of the finger almost to the tip;
   iii. While the fifth finger is "standing", the other fingers also lift, opening your hand;
   iv. Relax your hand and arm.

c) "Fall down" to create the sound on the accented notes. You should feel the sensation of falling, dropping, and release.

d) For the accented ♩ notes in mm. 10-11 and 13-14, continue to hold each note as you "stand up" to prepare the next note. Then "fall down" on the next ♩ note to create the sound, as above.

e) Return your hand to level and repeat the process.

Drills: G♭ Major

Drawbridge / Rotation Exercises

1. Preparation

Lift your arm about 3 inches above the key without bending at the wrist – as if it were a drawbridge. Flex your starting finger so it feels strong (in m.1, your fifth finger, in m.2 your fourth finger, etc.).

2. Sound Production

a) Play each whole note by dropping into the key, releasing your arm weight with energy. Your wrist should not drop below key level.

b) For each quarter note, without releasing the whole note:
  i. Rotate toward the finger holding the whole note;
  ii. Rotate back "down" into position, using this motion to create the sound;
  iii. Repeat for each quarter note.

3. Follow Through

Repeat from the beginning on each new whole note.

Upstroke / Inward Rotation Exercises

1. Preparation

Rest your hand on the surface of the keys in good position.

2. Sound Production

a) Play the first note and all the following pickup notes by gently swinging "in" to "stand up" on your thumb. The upward motion creates the sound on the pickup notes.

b) At the same time, rotate your hand towards the thumb to prepare for the accented notes:
  i. Your thumb position changes from parallel to the key to a comfortably upright position;
  ii. The end of the thumb rotates from the side of the thumb halfway to the tip;
  iii. While the thumb is "standing", the other fingers also lift, opening your hand;
  iv. Relax your hand and arm.

c) "Fall down" to create the sound on the accented notes. You should feel the sensation of falling, dropping, and release.

d) For the accented ♩ notes in mm. 10-11 and 13-14, continue to hold each note as you "stand up" to prepare the next note. Then "fall down" on the next ♩ note to create the sound, as above.

e) Return your hand to level and repeat the process.

No. 4

Upstroke / Outward Rotation Exercises

1. Preparation
Rest your hand on the surface of the keys in good position.

2. Sound Production

a) Play the first note and all the following pickup notes by swinging "in" to "stand up" on your fifth finger. The upward motion creates the sound on the pickup notes.

b) At the same time, rotate your hand towards the fifth finger to prepare for the accented notes:
   i. Your finger position changes from parallel to the key to a comfortably upright position;
   ii. The end of the finger rotates from the pad of the finger almost to the tip;

   iii. While the fifth finger is "standing", the other fingers also lift, opening your hand;
   iv. Relax your hand and arm.

c) "Fall down" to create the sound on the accented notes. You should feel the sensation of falling, dropping, and release.

d) For the accented ♩ notes in mm. 10-11 and 13-14, continue to hold each note as you "stand up" to prepare the next note. Then "fall down" on the next ♩ note to create the sound, as above.

e) Return your hand to level and repeat the process.

How to Use This Book

Many people consider Franz Liszt to be the greatest pianist who ever lived. He was a great believer in practicing technic. In his early years, he asked his students to spend two hours a day – on scales alone! This didn't include time spent on exercises, studies, or drills.

Most good pianists agree with Liszt; if you want to be good, you'll have to spend time practicing technic. In today's busy world, two hours a day on scales is too much for many students. But the more time you spend working on your technic, in every way, the better your playing will be.

Not sure how to proceed? The *American Popular Piano Technic* books are here to help!

The Learning Ladder

Initial Thoughts

Daily practice is essential. If you don't have a lot of time, work on your technic a little bit – but don't skip it!

■ Many teachers think you should do technical work for about 1/4 to 1/3 of your total practice time. It doesn't have to be done all at once. Some pianists like to work on technic at the beginning of a practice session, in order to warm up their fingers and their brain. Others prefer to do it later in the day, or to do several mini-sessions throughout the day. Experiment and see what works for you.

■ In general, it's better to repeat a smaller number of exercises many times, than to do lots of exercises a few times. Best, of course, is to do lots of exercises lots of times!

First Steps

Students often begin practicing the patterns hands separately. Play hands together when your teacher says you are ready.

■ Pick a key.
  1. Silently sing the exercise to yourself. Every detail of pitch, counting, and dynamics should be exact. Don't play until everything is clear in your mind.
  2. Play at a steady tempo without stopping. Aim for a tempo that is slow enough that everything is perfect.

■ Add a new key every few weeks, but don't forget to allow time for review of old keys.

■ Visit our website for other great ideas to vary your technical practice.

Checking

Technic is a visual, experiential and above all, a listening process.

■ Look.
  It's a good idea to memorize the basic technical patterns so you can look at your hands. (When sightreading and learning repertoire, it's a good idea **not** to look at your hands, but technical work is different).
  1. Make sure your hand position is good.

  2. Fingers should be in appropriate position, as directed. When not in preparation or use, they should be relaxed and close to the keys.
  3. Make sure hands mirror each other when completing the same movement. Hand position, degree of rotation, and finger placement should look the same in each hand.

■ Feel.
  It can be difficult, sometimes, to feel the difference between tension, which is bad, and flexion, which is necessary. A flexed finger feels strong – not stiff or claw-like. You should feel your finger relax after the note has been sounded. When you flex your fingers, check your shoulder, elbow, and wrist to make sure they are not clenched.

■ Listen.
  Good piano tone sounds rich, full, and resonant. Listen closely to make sure accented notes are strong, not "bangy".

Some Basic Tips

Audiate

Audiation is the ability to hear music in your mind without the presence of sound. It's a skill that all good musicians must possess. So "audiate" before you play. Don't start playing without singing silently to yourself. Then, play and try to match the sound you created in your brain.

Slow Practice

The surest path to brilliant, fast technic is controlled, repetitive practice at a deliberate, slow tempo. Spend a significant portion of your time practicing slowly. Listen carefully and check carefully.

■ Is every note rhythmically exact? All quarter notes should be precisely the same length. Whole notes should be exactly four times as long as quarter notes. Are yours?

■ Does every note have a full, rounded tone quality?

■ Are all the notes tonally even? You shouldn't hear some notes lighter or more full than others. Liszt told his students that nothing should ever be abrupt or uneven. Pay special attention to your thumb!

■ Are you playing at the correct dynamic? Are all notes dynamically matched? No notes should sound "thumping" or, conversely, too soft in relation to the others.

Repetition

There are many opinions about the optimal number of times to practice. For us, the magic number is "5". 5 times is the basic number of repetitions, do 10 times for a good workout, and play 15 times for the greatest effectiveness. An important factor in improving fundamentals is: **work on them—and do it often!!**

The root word for technic is the ancient Greek tekhnikos – "about art". So practice these excerpts with full artistry and with love. Let the fact that they are musically simple help you focus your full attention on the technical challenges. Repeat often, concentrate — and listen closely! Your diligence will be rewarded.